CW00419484

OPTIMIZE YOUR DAY

UNLEASH THE POWER OF YOUR MORNINGS

DANA RONGIONE

CONTENTS

CHAPTER ONE

INTRODUCTION

The morning sun had just begun to rise over the distant horizon, soft pink and yellow hues painting the sky with a pastel-like beauty. I sat on my porch, cup of hot tea in hand, enjoying the peaceful atmosphere that surrounded me as I prepared to start my day.

My new morning routine was something I found important to maintain a sense of balance in my life. It allowed me to start the day with intention, refocusing my thoughts away from the mundane and toward the incredible potential that each day held.

In my hand, I held my pen and *Optimize Your Day Journal*. I opened my journal and began the process that was the key to starting my days off on the right foot. I had learned to adopt a more contemplative approach to beginning my day, taking time to listen, reflect, and respond to the Lord. This soon became a form of meditation for me, a way to not just read but to really take time to consider God's Word and how it applied to my life.

As I read, my thoughts were drawn away from the hustle and bustle of everyday life and into a place of stillness and peace. Here, I was reminded of God's promises and was encouraged to live life with an abundance of faith and hope.

Finishing my time of optimization, I stood and stretched my arms toward the sky. I breathed in the fresh morning air, content with the knowledge that I had done something that would equip me for the day ahead. And with that, I was ready to start the day.

W e all need a jumpstart to get our day going in the right direction. That's why I developed the *Optimize Your Day* routine: a system for getting into God's Word and setting our focus on Him first thing in the morning, every morning. This isn't just some chore to add to our already hectic list of things to do. Instead, it is a tool that offers a sense of peace and starts our days off with clarity and direction. It clears away all the noise and chaos in our lives and reminds us to focus on what truly matters.

As C.S. Lewis put it in his book, *Mere Christianity*, "The moment you wake up each morning, all your wishes and hopes for the day rush at you like wild animals. And the first job each morning consists in shoving them all back; in listening to that other voice, taking that other point of view, letting that other larger, stronger, quieter life come flowing in." That's what *Optimize Your Day* is all about. Let's dive in so you can reap its incredible benefits!

This process should take thirty minutes at maximum unless you plan to make this your daily devotion time as well, in which case, it may be longer. Take some time with each step in the routine. Make sure to do them all in order as they build upon each other. You might grasp specific steps immediately, yet others may need more explanation. A few will produce instant results, while the rest may take more time to bear fruit. What's important is to stick with it.

In this book, you'll discover the OPTIMIZE method, a powerful acrostic that outlines the key steps to a morning routine that will optimize every area of your life:

Organization: Start your day with a clear plan and maximize your productivity.

Prayer: Connect with the Lord to find strength and guidance.

Thanksgiving: Cultivate an attitude of gratitude and abundance.

Illumination: Seek wisdom and insights from the Word that light your path to success.

Meditation: Achieve a clearer, more personal understanding of God's Word.

Inscription: Put your thoughts in writing to solidify them in your mind.

Zeroing In: Set meaningful intentions for the day ahead.

Exercise: Energize your body and mind for a healthy and vibrant life.

Throughout this book, I'll go through each step of the routine in detail and explain its advantages. Like me, I'm sure you'll find that following such a routine at the start of your day will help keep God and His goodness in focus. What makes *Optimize Your Day* great is that you do it before performing any other activity. Doing so helps ensure that the spiritual aspect of your life always comes first.

When breakfast time or work hours come around, you feel empowered knowing that you have completed a task that will help make the day more successful. Armed with this sense of accomplishment and the tools you need, you can stride out into the world, ready to face anything that comes your way.

C *ause me to hear thy lovingkindness in the morning; for in thee do I trust: cause me to know the way wherein I should walk; for I lift up my soul unto thee. - Psalm 143:8*

CHAPTER TWO

ORGANIZATION

I don't know about you, but when I first wake up, my mind is a whirlwind of lists and demands. Before I can even pry my eyes open, my brain is going through the day's inventory of tasks, appointments, and requirements. It's a bit overwhelming as I try to sort through the many thoughts and make mental notes to remember this and that.

This is where the first step of optimizing our day begins. Let's get that clutter out of our minds so we can focus on the other tasks and start the day in peace. It's time to *Organize*.

My entire optimization process takes place in my office because that works best for me. You can choose whatever location works best for you. Just ensure it's quiet, and you can have a few minutes undisturbed. Ideally, you'll stay in this one location for your entire optimization process.

For this first step, you'll need a calendar, appointment book, notepad, or one of my *Optimize Your Day Journals* to organize your thoughts and time. Take a few minutes to plan your day, making sure you write down anything you need to remember to do (even if it doesn't have a specified time). This doesn't have to be exact or detailed. It's just a process to clear your mind productively. Let the thoughts flow. Get it all out.

Do you need to order groceries? Add it to the list. Does your child have a music lesson at 4:00? Write it down. Did you remember your mom's birthday and want to call her later? Great! Put it down on your notes. You can even plan your meals for the day so your thoughts aren't occupied with what you're going to eat later. Whether it's related to family, work, church, or anything else, write it down.

This may seem like a frivolous process, but I want you to know it works. I've discovered my mind is so much clearer and more focused when I'm not trying to hold onto all these bits of information. By writing it down, I can be assured I won't forget it, and with that knowledge, I can temporarily release it from my mind. It's on the list. It will get done, but not right now.

Once you've crafted a plan for your day and organized your thoughts, it's time to move on to the next step—*Prayer.*

*L*et all things be done decently and in order. - I Corinthians 14:40

CHAPTER THREE

PRAYER

U nless you are using this time for your daily devotions, this is not intended to be your primary
prayer time. You can take care of that whenever it suits
your schedule, but this is just a few quiet minutes with
God. Remember, the entire *Optimize Your Day* program
should take no more than thirty minutes (unless it's also
your daily devotion time), so don't feel you need to cram
all your prayer requests into this small time frame. That's
not what this is about. It's not about asking for things.
It's all about starting your day in the arms of the Savior.

This personal time is between you and God, so I won't
presume to tell you what you should say. I will say that
I typically use this time to dedicate myself and my day
to the Lord. I thank Him for a good night's sleep and
another day to serve Him. Then I ask Him to use me in

a mighty way throughout the day. The words and the message change a little from day to day, depending on my mood and the current state of my heart, but for the most part, this is time for me to remember why I'm here and who I serve. Getting that straight in my head and heart before I begin the day is vital to my physical, spiritual, mental, and emotional health.

As with the words, your posture during this process is entirely up to you. You can kneel on the floor, sit in a chair, or recline on the couch. You do what feels right and what you feel the Lord would have you do. The most important thing now is to rid your mind of all distractions (which we did during the *Organize* phase) and focus solely on Jesus. This is His time!

Here's my favorite part of this entire program. Let's say that you were planning to pray while fixing breakfast, but your five-year-old lost her shoe, the one she had to wear to school that day, and you spent the morning searching for said shoe, leaving you with no option but to hand each of the kids a Pop-tart as you headed out the door. *No problem*, you think. *I'll use my lunch break to catch up on my prayer time.* But your boss has another idea, and you spend your lunch break in a business meeting. The day goes on, and every opportunity to grab some quiet time with the Lord somehow backfires. By the end of the day, you finally have some time, but you're exhausted in every way possible. Doesn't it make you feel good knowing you've already spent time with the Lord? Sure, you wanted to do more. I get that. But at least the day didn't rob you of every opportunity. By making this your priority of the day, nothing else can steal it away.

Because of this, I recommend getting up about 30 minutes earlier than the rest of your household. That way, you can have this time all to yourself. No distractions!

Prayer is a powerful thing. Ideally, we'll spend more than a few minutes praying each day. But, at the very least, begin your day by talking to the Lord. He deserves our time and attention more than anyone else, so it's only fitting that He gets our attention first. That way, too, He gets our best, not what's left after a hard, frustrating day.

*M*y voice shalt thou hear in the morning, O Lord; in the morning will I direct my prayer unto thee, and will look up. - Psalm 5:3

CHAPTER FOUR

THANKSGIVING

We all know we should be grateful for the many blessings the Lord has given us. But I want to impress upon you the importance of beginning our day with gratitude. Many things will make us want to fuss, gripe, or maybe even cry. That's life. But by beginning our day with a focus on our blessings, it's much easier to overlook or deal with life's frustrations. By starting with gratitude, we can circumvent that mindset that cries, "Nothing good ever happens to me!"

There are so many things to be thankful for, and throughout the day, we should thank the Lord for as many things as possible, whether it be the close parking space on a rainy day or the excellent report at the doctor's office. Big things. Little things. We need to consider how much God is doing in our lives.

But during your morning optimization, narrow your thanks down to one thing, preferably different than the days before. Why just one thing? Because it's easy for us to generalize things in our minds and allow the thoughts to pass through without really taking them in. In a sense, we begin to recite a list. "I'm thankful for my salvation and my family and my house and church and..." But as we're reciting, are we giving thanks for those things, or are we simply stating the facts because we know we should be thankful for all those things? By narrowing it down to one thing per day, we force our minds to think about and focus on that one thing. Why am I thankful for this? How has it impacted my life? How can I use this blessing to impact the lives of others? Do you see how difficult it would be to do that with an entire list?

So, for your morning optimization, pick one thing you are genuinely grateful for. As strange as it may seem, I've found that there's usually something specific on my heart that I want to thank the Lord for that particular day. I don't have to think about it. It's almost like I woke up with it on my mind. For example, one of my big book promotions went well yesterday, and my book surpassed two of the top authors in the field. That excited me when I saw the results last night, so naturally, when I awoke this morning, those happy thoughts were still with me. During my *Thanksgiving* time this morning, I praised the

Lord for the high rankings on my book and for all the people who, I hope, will receive a blessing from the book.

What you choose to thank the Lord for is entirely up to you, but I think you will also find that the Lord will place something on your heart. It doesn't have to be a big thing. It may seem insignificant, especially to someone else, but that doesn't matter. If it's important to you, it's important to God, so thank Him. Fill your heart with gratitude for Who He is and what He's done! And when you've done that, you can move on to the next step—*Illumination.*

*E*nter into his gates with thanksgiving, and into his courts with praise: be thankful unto him, and bless his name. - *Psalm 100:4*

CHAPTER FIVE

ILLUMINATION

L et's talk about the fourth step in optimizing our mornings, and that step is *Illumination.* To illuminate something is to shed light on it. That is precisely what we'll do each morning. Once our thoughts are organized, and after our moments of prayer and thanksgiving, we will add some light to our day by reading a short passage to focus our hearts and minds on the Lord. After all, Psalm 119:105 says, *Thy word is a lamp unto my feet, and a light unto my path.*

Remember, like your morning prayer, this may or may not be your primary devotion time. If it's not, you can accomplish that later in the day. For now, this is something short to, once again, get your focus on God. It can be a verse, a short passage of Scripture, or even a short devotional that brings out an application from a particular part of the Bible. If you're using my *Optimize Your Day Journals*, each day includes a verse of Scripture and an accompanying devotional.

When you start your day, try to focus on God's greatness. Don't treat this activity as if it's just a task on your schedule. Listen and try to discern what God is trying to tell you. Pay close attention.

What you read is up to you, but here are a few suggestions to help you get started:

Psalm 23

Read one verse per day, or read the entire passage for several days in a row to let it sink in.

The Names of God

Focus each day on reading a passage about a particular name or character trait of God. For example, in Psalm 23, He is our Shepherd. In Genesis 17, we see Him as El-Shaddai (God Almighty). Genesis 22 portrays God as Jehovah-Jireh (God the provider). You can find a list of these names and passages online or purchase a book with them. Read the passage or passages related to a particular name or attribute each day and allow the light of Who God is to shine down on you.

The Book of Psalms

This is my favorite book of the Bible. Though written thousands of years ago, I find them so relevant to my current circumstances and emotions. Most psalms are pretty short, and they all have something that will bless and encourage you.

The Gospels

The first four books of the New Testament are filled with fantastic stories of Who God is and what He's capable of. Read a chapter at a time, or if you have a study Bible, the chapters will be divided into individual stories you can read daily.

There's a Verse for That

Please forgive the shameless plug, but if you want to focus on verses by topic, you might enjoy using this book as a guide. It includes verses for varying circumstances, like feeling alone, afraid, discouraged, or confused. Read one verse or a few until something jumps out at you.

Giggles and Grace Devotional Series

While I'm doing shameless plugs, I might also mention this series. If you're unfamiliar with these books, they are full of short devotionals that focus on a verse and an application of that verse. Most of these devotions can be read in less than five minutes.

Optimize Your Day Journals

I'll be honest. I created these journals for myself as I discovered it to be the simplest way to have everything I need in one convenient location. As I mentioned, each day includes a verse of Scripture and an original devotional, plus everything else you need for your morning optimization process.

These are just a few ideas. I'm sure you probably have others. Perhaps you have a devotional guide by your favorite author. That's fine. The idea is to read something that will bring light and encouragement to your day and help bring (and keep) your focus on God. In the next chapter, we'll take this reading a step further, so be sure to keep reading.

F or whatsoever things were written aforetime were written for our learning, that we through patience and comfort of the scriptures might have hope. – Romans 15:4

CHAPTER SIX

MEDITATION

So far, we've discussed the first four steps of optimizing our day: Organization, Prayer, Thanksgiving, and Illumination. Our next action—*Meditation*—picks up where our morning reading left off. It's time to do more than just read. We need to meditate on what we've read.

Meditation is the act of thinking or pondering. It goes beyond just mouthing the words and allows the message of those words to penetrate the mind and heart. One of the most familiar illustrations of meditation is that of a cow chewing its cud. To meditate on a portion of Scripture essentially means to chew on it and chew on it and chew on it until you get all the "goodie" out of it.

Here are a few questions you can ask to help you meditate on your reading:

(1) What did I just read? (Summarize)

(2) What is this passage saying in general? (What is the interpretation?)

(3) What is this passage saying to me? (What is the application?)

(4) How can this passage strengthen or encourage me in my daily walk with the Lord?

(5) Is there anything else I can glean from this Scripture?

(6) Do any other related verses come to my mind?

(7) What does this passage tell me about God?

Don't feel you need to answer every question or are limited to those seven questions. The point is to allow the Scripture to become more than words. The Bible is alive and can work powerfully in our lives if we let it. Ponder the verses. Take them to heart. Allow God to speak to you through them. You may be amazed at what you see!

I haven't counted them, but I think it's safe to say there are probably hundreds of verses about meditation in the Bible, but I want to share one of my favorites with you. Psalm

143:5 says, *I remember the days of old; I meditate on all thy works; I muse on the work of thy hands.*

That's just so poetic, and as the creative type, I love the word "muse." As a verb, it means "meditate, ponder, contemplate, chew on," but as a noun, it means "inspiration." How appropriate! Meditating on the Word of God inspires us to live our days for His glory. It encourages us to focus on Him, who He is, and what He's done. That inspiration can linger with us throughout the day because we take the time to hide God's Word in our hearts.

It's exciting, isn't it? But before you get too carried away, let me remind you that we're not done yet. There's more to come, and just as it has been with each step, the next one builds off of this one, which is why it's essential to do these in order.

M y meditation of him shall be sweet: I will be glad in the Lord. - Psalm 104:34

CHAPTER SEVEN

INSCRIPTION

The second "I" in optimize stands for *Inscription,* which is just a fancy word for writing. Yes, I'm talking about journaling. Some of the most successful and productive people use a journal. I think that we, as Christians, ought to seek to be just as successful and effective in our daily walk with Christ, so journaling is a definite must.

I know what some of you are saying. "Sure, Dana, that's easy for you to say. You're a writer. I can't write. I don't like to write. My spelling and grammar are horrible!" I'm not talking about writing a book here, and it doesn't matter what your spelling and grammar are like because no one will read this but you. It's your private journal, and what it contains is between you and God.

So, the first thing you'll want to do is decide on a medium for your journal. You can use a plain spiral notebook, a fancy leather journal, an *Optimize Your Day Journal*, or if you're more comfortable with a keyboard, you can set up a private blog for your morning thoughts. It doesn't matter. What is important is that you're happy with the setup.

Once you've chosen your journaling method, commit to writing/typing something in it every morning. So, what are you supposed to write during this time? Anything! You can write down the Bible verse you read that morning or the thoughts you were meditating on. You can write out your worries and fears to get them out of your heart and mind and then commit them to God. Write down what you're feeling. Write down what God lays on your heart. Write down what you're thankful for.

It's entirely up to you, but there's something about jour-naling that helps clear the mind. It's a little weird how it works. I've found that writing down the negative things I'm feeling gets it out of my system like I've poured them out onto the page. Then I don't feel the power of them anymore.

But, when I write down something positive (like what I'm thankful for or my daily verse), the writing process reinforces that thought in my brain, making it easier to access throughout the day. Strange, huh? But, honestly, this is what I've discovered about journaling, so I urge you to try it.

If you're stumped at first and need help figuring out what to write, try jotting down a recent blessing or your favorite verse. You may find that the words start spilling out from there. Another thing to keep in mind is that it doesn't matter how much you write each day as long as you write something. It can be a sentence, a paragraph, a page, or more. And what you write today doesn't have to be the same thing you wrote yesterday. Perhaps yesterday, you wrote down some thoughts weighing heavy on your mind. You don't have to do that again today if you don't want to. Today, you could inscribe your meditations. There is so much freedom here, and it can be an enjoyable process if you allow it to be.

In the next chapter, we'll talk about another step in the process, which may also be something you want to write about, so you see, the possibilities are endless. Before then, decide on your journaling method and pour your thoughts onto paper (or computer). Come on, give it a try!

*M*y heart is inditing a good matter: I speak of the things which I have made touching the king: my tongue is the pen of a ready writer. - Psalm 45:1

CHAPTER EIGHT

ZEROING IN

I f you've been following along in the process, you know
now that the steps of optimizing your day build upon
one another. Our next action is no different. Up to this
point, we've organized our thoughts and said a quick
prayer to dedicate ourselves and our day to the Lord.
We've given thanks for a particular thing. We've read and
meditated on Scripture and written down some of our
innermost thoughts. Now, we're going to take all of that
and *Zero In* on how each of those things can impact our
day by asking ourselves this question: "Armed with the
knowledge I've gained this morning and the thoughts the
Lord has laid on my heart, in what specific ways can I
serve the Lord today?"

Remember, the key here is to zero in, which means we're
not going to give a general answer like, "I will strive to do

good and resist temptation." No, that's not going to do it. At this point, you need to look at your day, agenda, and plans for that day and set actionable goals to serve God in specific ways based on your daily schedule.

For example, let's say your reading and meditation this morning involved a passage about praise, and the Lord laid it on your heart that you need to worship Him more. Then, you look at your daily schedule and find that many things on it cause you to grumble and complain. Right there, you can stop and say, "I am deciding right now to find something to praise God for during these tough spots in my day. I won't gripe or whine but will keep my heart focused on God and how worthy He is of my praise."

Or you could look at your schedule and see that you're expected to spend most of the day around someone who gets on your nerves. Decide that you're going to do your best (God working in and through you) to show the love of God to that person and to bestow grace on that person even though you may not think they deserve it because you are reminded that God shows you grace every day when you don't deserve it.

As a final example, I'll share what the Lord laid on my heart Sunday morning during my optimization. He's been working in my heart about giving more and expecting less, so Sunday morning, as I looked at my busy day, filled mostly with church activities, I made a decision. I would serve the Lord with gladness, giving unto others as much as possible and expecting nothing in return. Anytime during the day that I began to feel overwhelmed or irritable, the Lord brought to mind my goal, and I thanked Him and continued the service without ill feelings. The difference was phenomenal, and it felt so good to do for others with a right spirit instead of "grudgingly or of necessity." (II Corinthians 9:7)

I don't know what your days may hold, and I can't say what the Lord will impress on your heart. But whatever it is, be specific. The more specific you are, the more likely your goal will stick with you throughout the day and imprint on your heart and mind. And don't kill yourself trying to come up with something. I can't think of a single time when I looked at my schedule and God didn't immediately point out some area where I could "zero in" on my service to Him. The process takes a few minutes, but the impact will last throughout the day.

Philippians 2:12 tells us, *Wherefore, my beloved, as ye have always obeyed, not as in my presence only, but now much more in my absence, work out your own salvation with fear and trembling.*

This passage is not saying that we have to work for our salvation. It is telling that God has done a good work in us, and we need to let it work its way to the outside so that others can see. In other words, we work because we're saved. Zeroing in is taking the message God put in our hearts and putting it into action throughout our day. It's good to know the things of God, but it's even better to do them. That's what this step is all about.

In what specific ways can you serve God today?

CHAPTER NINE

EXERCISE

W hew! It's been a long journey, but we've finally arrived at the last step in *Optimize Your Day: Exercise.* Not only does exercise benefit our bodies, but it also helps increase our focus and improve our overall attitude. But let me stress that this is not (and should not be) the only exercise you get throughout the day (unless you have the time to devote to it now). Otherwise, this is simply a quick boost to get your body moving, your blood flowing, and your mind awake. I like to focus on an exercise session between five and ten minutes long.

Okay, so what kind of exercises should you do? That's entirely up to you. If you have an exercise bike, treadmill, or elliptical, you may want to do 5-10 minutes of cardio. That's fine. If you're a fan of Pilates, YouTube has an impressive selection of quick videos that can lead you through a brief morning workout. You can walk around your neighborhood or do 100 jumping jacks. If you have joint issues that make getting out of bed in the morning difficult, ten minutes or so of gentle stretches can do wonders!

The possibilities are endless, and determining what works best for you may take a few tries. Some of you may enjoy the same daily routine, while others want more variety. That's fine! You know your needs, your body's limitations, and what you like, so implement that knowledge.

What are you trying to accomplish during this time? As I said, this is not your main workout, so the focus shouldn't be on calories burned or weight loss. This time is about waking up your body and loosening your joints. Even a brief morning routine can allow additional oxygen to the body, which helps us to shake off the grogginess, focus our minds, and improve our attitudes. I know some of you will balk at this, but a five-minute workout in the morning will give you more boost than a cup of coffee. (That's not to say you can't have the coffee, too. Okay? Please don't hate me!)

One last thing I want to address in this area is the plethora of excuses people can devise for not exercising. There are no good reasons to ignore the care of the temple of the Holy Ghost! Sorry, but it's true. Are there factors that limit the amount or types of exercise some are capable of? Absolutely. If all you can do is ten toe touches and five knee bends, that's fine. Do that! But please, don't allow excuses to hinder you from getting your day off on the right foot. You'll be amazed at how much better and more energetic you'll feel after just a few minutes of exercise. Try it and see!

Whatever exercise you decide to do, make it fun! One of my favorite things to do is to play worship music during this time. That way, I'm still focused on God instead of myself, and it makes the exercise time a lot easier. Some days, I want to keep going because I enjoy the music so much.

Remember, this is the last step of our morning optimization. By this point, we've filled our minds and hearts with thoughts of God. We've prayed, given thanks, read and meditated on the Word of God, and set up a plan for honoring God throughout the day. Don't allow all that positive energy to go out the window by thinking, Great! Now I have to exercise. I hate exercise! Instead, think of it as a service to the Lord. By caring for your body, you can do more for the Lord and others. Keep that in mind as you're working out, and it will help keep negativity at bay.

That's it! Those are the eight steps to *Optimize Your Day* each morning, every day. In the final chapter, I'll briefly review the steps and give an example of a complete morning optimization.

What? know ye not that your body is the temple of the Holy Ghost which is in you, which ye have of God, and ye are not your own? – I Corinthians 6:19

CHAPTER TEN

CONCLUSION

I hope you've enjoyed this book about getting your day off to a good start and have already begun implementing what you've learned. Before we come to the end, though, I wanted to take a few minutes to look back over the entire process. Let's go!

Organization

Before anything else, clear your mind of all the day's demands. Write down any random thoughts and schedule out your plans for the day. This allows you to focus on the rest of the process. Should another thought or reminder pop up during the remainder of your optimize time, jot it down and let it go for the time being.

Prayer

Spend a few minutes dedicating yourself and your day to the Lord. Be brief but specific. Just let the Lord know how much you love Him.

Thanksgiving

Pick one thing each day to be grateful for and spend a few moments thanking the Lord for that thing. Specify what it means to you, why you're thankful, etc. Again, be specific, but don't let it take up too much time. If you're specific, I guarantee you'll be thinking about it on and off all day long.

Illumination

Read a Bible verse, Bible passage, or a short devotion based on a Bible verse.

Meditation

Chew on the verse, passage, or devotion you read. Think about how it applies to your life in general. What can you take away from it?

Inscription

Spend a few minutes journaling about anything God has laid on your heart. You can write out your verse, jot down your meditation thoughts, lay out a burden on your heart, or anything else. It doesn't matter what you write during this time as long as it is God-focused.

Zeroing in

Put together all the pieces of your morning routine and focus on how to practice them during your day. Think specifically about your schedule for that particular day and how you can serve God based on what He put on your heart that morning.

Exercise

Do 5-10 minutes of exercise—whether it be walking, strength training, or merely stretching—to get your body moving, your blood flowing, and your oxygen levels up.

To ensure we're all on the same page, here's an example of one of my morning *OPTIMIZE* routines.

6:30 – I pulled out my *Optimize Your Day Journal* and reviewed the events of the day. I jotted down a couple of reminders that had come to mind during the night.

6:32 – I prayed. While I didn't write down my exact prayer, it went like this: "Good morning, Lord. Thank you for a good night's sleep and another day to serve you. Today is my writing day, and I ask you to please guide my thoughts as I work. Help me to write only what you would have me to, and may the message that comes forth be a blessing to all who read it. Keep my heart and mind focused on you today, I pray. I love you! Amen."

6:35 – I thanked the Lord for the opportunity to begin a new writing project. I expressed my excitement about the process and gratitude for having the health, time, and ability to write another book that would spread the message of God's Word and ultimately bring glory to Him. I wrote this down in my journal.

6:38 – I read today's verse and devotion from my *Optimize Your Day Journal*.

6:43 – I meditated on both the verse and the devotion, seeing how they went together and also how they applied to my life.

6:46 - I jotted down the verse and my meditations on that verse. Then I went ahead and wrote down my zero in because I like to reflect on it later.

6:50 - Today, I am working in my office, so I reminded myself that no matter how the day goes, the Lord is with me. He has my back and is in control of everything; therefore, I can go about my day without worry or fear, and, in the process, I can be a testimony to others by sharing God's promise with them.

6:54 - I pulled up a YouTube video of a 5-minute morning stretching routine. After rolling out my yoga mat, I completed the short workout.

7:00 - After making a cup of hot tea, I sat down at my desk feeling revived, rejuvenated, and in touch with the Lord. I started my writing process. That's it!

Mornings are the perfect time to focus on God's presence and align our intentions with His. Like any new habit, it takes practice. Still, eventually, we can find ourselves looking forward to each morning as an opportunity to serve Him. Start today by beginning a routine that focuses on Him and let Him lead you through the rest of the day! By taking these small steps each morning, you can seize the day and live out your faith authentically.

Overall, having a God-focused morning routine is essential to having a successful day. It helps us remain rooted in faith so that we can overcome any obstacles that may come our way throughout the day with grace and poise because we know that no matter what happens, He will always be there beside us to guide us through every step!

This is the day which the Lord hath made; we will rejoice and be glad in it. - Psalm 118:24

CHAPTER ELEVEN

OPTIMIZE YOUR DAY JOURNALS

Introducing the Complete "Optimize Your Day" Monthly Journals – Your Path to Daily Transformation!

Tired of juggling multiple journals, planners, and devotional guides to kickstart your day with purpose? Discover the all-in-one solution to elevate your daily routine and reach new heights of productivity, mindfulness, and spiritual growth.

One Book, Endless Transformation: With my Monthly Journals, you can effortlessly follow the life-changing "Optimize Your Day" program all year round, right within the pages of a single journal. Say goodbye to clutter and confusion!

Optimize Your Every Day: Each Monthly Journal is thoughtfully crafted to include dedicated sections for every step of the "Optimize Your Day" process, including Organization, Prayer, Thanksgiving, Illumination, Meditation, Inscription, Zeroing In, and Exercise. Your entire day's journey, all in one place.

Daily Devotions for Spiritual Renewal: Experience a unique blend of daily devotions tailored to align your heart, mind, and soul with the truth of God's Word. Start your mornings with purpose and a stronger connection with the Lord.

A Month of Growth, One Journal: Forget about switching between numerous books! I've got you covered. My Monthly Journals ensure that you always have the guidance and space you need to focus on your daily intentions.

Transform Your Life: Whether you're aiming for increased productivity, greater spiritual alignment, or enhanced mindfulness, the "Optimize Your Day" Monthly Journals will guide you on this transformational journey.

Experience the convenience of a clutter-free, comprehensive journal that takes you through the "Optimize Your Day" program seamlessly. Get your Monthly Journals today and embark on a year of daily renewal and growth like never before. Your path to transformation begins here! For more information, visit DanaRongione.com.

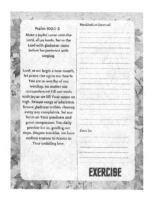

ABOUT THE AUTHOR

Meet Dana Rongione, the Christian author who's on a mission to turn worriers into warriors one encouraging word at a time.

With her trusty terrier, Tess, and her husband, Jason, by her side, Dana has traded the sunny streets of Greenville, SC, for the enchanting landscapes of Wales, where they dedicate themselves to chapel ministries.

When Dana's not busy teaching her beloved Bible study group or working on her latest book, you'll likely find her reading in a cozy nook while sipping on a steaming cup of chamomile, lemon balm, or yerba mate tea. Her love for chocolate knows no bounds, and her quirky sense of humor is always close at hand, ready to add a touch of whimsy to life's moments.

But there's a deeper side to Dana. She's no stranger to the challenges of anxiety, depression, and chronic illness, and it's this very journey that fuels her passion for helping others find strength in the midst of life's storms.

Join Dana on her quest to enjoy God more fully. Explore her collection of Christian books, including the cherished "Giggles and Grace" devotional series for women, and dive into a world where faith, humor, and a cup of tea can work wonders.

Connect with Dana at DanaRongione.com, and don't forget to sign up for her devotional blog and subscribe to her YouTube Channel.

ALSO BY DANA RONGIONE

Christian Living

Rise Up and Build Series: A Biblical Way to Dealing with Anxiety and Depression

- Rise Up and Build

- Rise Up and Build Study Guide

- Rise Up and Build Devotional

- Rise Up and Build Good Health

He's Still Working Miracles

There's a Verse for That

The Deadly Darts of the Devil

What Happened to Prince Charming?

<u>Devotional</u>

Giggle and Grace Daily Devotionals for Women

- Random Ramblings of a Raving Redhead

- Daily Discussions of a Doubting Disciple

- Lilting Laments of a Looney Lass

- Mindful Musings of a Moody Motivator

Books for Children

The Delaware Detectives: Middle–Grade Mystery Series

- The Delaware Detectives

- Through Many Dangers

- My Fears Relieved

- I Once Was Lost

Through the Eyes of a Child

God Can Use My Differences

Printed in Great Britain
by Amazon